Playmakers

Power Forwards

Lynn M. Stone

Rourke

Publishing LLC
Vero Beach, Florida 32964

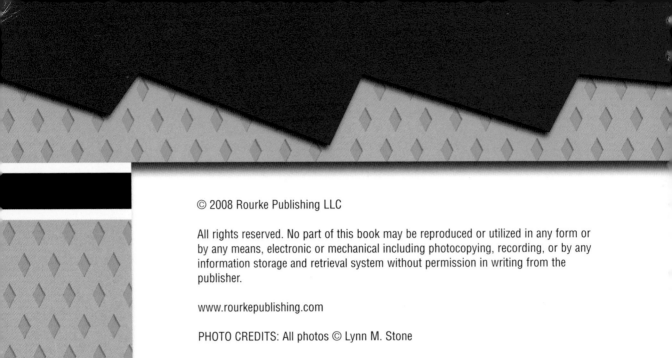

www.rourkepublishing.com

PHOTO CREDITS: All photos © Lynn M. Stone

Editor: Robert Stengard-Olliges

Cover and page design by Tara Raymo

Library of Congress Cataloging-in-Publication Data

Stone, Lynn M.
  Power forwards / Lynn Stone.
    p. cm. -- (Playmakers)
  ISBN 978-1-60044-595-8
  1. Forwards (Basketball)--Juvenile literature. 2. Basketball--Offense--Juvenile literature. I. Title.
  GV889.S76 2008
  796.323--dc22
                                    2007022533

Printed in the USA

CG/CG

Rourke Publishing

www.rourkepublishing.com – rourke@rourkepublishing.com
Post Office Box 3328, Vero Beach, FL 32964

2

Table of Contents

Power Forwards

A power forward is a power position. It requires the player to work hard under the basket for **rebounds**, both at the offensive and defensive ends of a court. The ideal power forward is an athlete combining both strength and size. The power forward generally sets up near the basket. The power forward is typically not as tall as a team's center, but he or she is very likely to be stronger than the players at other positions.

Forwards usually play close to the baskets.

Other Forwards

Basketball teams take the floor with five players each. Each of the players has a position on the court. Two of those players were once simply known as forwards. Today, the forwards are better known as a "small" forward and a "power" forward, or as the "three" and "four" respectively.

Both of these middle school forwards are about 6 feet (1.5 meters) tall.

A small forward (left) especially tends to be a good shooter and an active, highly athletic player.

As the term "small" suggests, the small forward tends to be smaller than a power forward. At the same time, both forwards are typically larger than a basketball team's **guards**. The team's **center** is generally the largest player.

The best small forwards can dribble and drive as well as shoot, rebound, and pass the basketball.

Small forwards are counted on for rebounding, too, but not to the extent that power forwards and centers are.

Like any player on the court, small forwards are also counted on for defense. A tall, athletic small forward tends to be one of the most **versatile** defenders on the floor. They can often switch from guarding another small forward to a larger opponent. And because of their athletic ability, small forwards can also switch to cover an opposing guard. A perfect example is former Chicago Bulls all-star and small forward Scottie Pippen.

Working for position, a forward on defense "boxes out" his opponent from the lane under the basket.

Power forwards score many baskets from short range, including layups and slam dunks.

Grappling for rebounds is just part of a forward's job.

A skilled small forward is a good passer, scorer, and rebounder. With that skill set, the small forward may also be called upon to play shooting guard at times. A shooting guard, the so-called two-spot, tends to roam further from the basket than a forward. By playing at the shooting guard position the player won't be in position to rebound as often as he or she might have at the three position. But in addition to scoring more, a small forward shifted to shooting guard may also have a chance to pass the ball more and collect **assists**.

So, You Want to Be a Power Forward?

Most power forwards don't have the shooting touch of guards and the small forward, nor are they usually in a position to score from "outside." They are the worker bees, the players "in the trenches" who work underneath the baskets. The most effective power forwards gain favorable position through their technique and strength to capture rebounds. Because of their close-to-the-basket work, power forwards tend to score many of their points on short shots. Power forwards and centers are a team's least likely three-point shooters.

The rebound often goes to the player who has established the best position near the basket and who is the most aggressive.

Forwards jockey for inside position for a rebound...

...but having inside position doesn't guarantee a rebound if the ball skips far off the rim.

On offense, the power forward typically plays with his or her back to the basket. The power forward is not required to dribble the ball often, but the four-spot does require some passing, often from the inside (close to the basket) back to a guard or small forward away from the basket.

A power forward, back to the basket, "posts up" his opponent.

In a man-to-man defense, the power forward typically guards the opponent's power forward. In a zone defense, the power forward sets up to one side of the basket and fairly close to it.

In man-to-man defense, one forward tries to stick to the opponent like a glove.

Glossary

assists (uh SISSTZ) – a basketball pass that leads directly to a basket by a member of the passing player's team

center (SEN tur) – the "five" position on a basketball team; usually a team's tallest player and the one counted on for shot blocking, rebounding, and close-in baskets

fouled (FOULD) – a player whose on-court movement has in some way been physically hampered in an illegal way by an opposing player; to commit a foul as called by a referee

free throw (FREE THROH) – a point, or the attempt of scoring a point, from a set line, after a player has been fouled by an opponent

guards (GARDZ) – two basketball positions generally requiring the most passing and ball handling skills

rebound (REE bound) – a successful grab of a basketball after a missed shot at the basket

versatile (VUR suh tuhl) – having the ability to do many things

Index

Further Reading

Baskin, Nora. *Basketball*. Trophy Books, 2007.
Drewett, Jim. *How to Improve at Basketball*. Crabtree Publishing, 2007.
Ramen, Fred. *Basketball: Rules, Tips, Strategy, and Safety*. Rosen, 2007.

Website to Visit

http://answers.com/topic/basketball-position
http://www.guidetocoachingbasketball.com/motion.htm

About the Author

Lynn M. Stone is the author of more than 400 children's books. He is a talented natural history photographer as well. Lynn, a former teacher, travels worldwide to photograph wildlife in its natural habitat.